ruth and esther

the books of

ruth
and esther

authorised king james version

printed by authority

published by canongate

with an introduction by | joanna trollope

First published in Great Britain in 1999
by Canongate Books Ltd
14 High Street, Edinburgh EH1 1TE

10 9 8 7 6 5 4 3 2 1

Introduction copyright © Joanna Trollope 1999
The moral right of the author has been asserted

British Library Cataloguing-in-Publication Data
A catalogue record is available on request from
the British Library

ISBN 0 86241 968 9

Typeset by Palimpsest Book Production
Book design by Paddy Cramsie at et al
Printed and bound in Great Britain
by Caledonian International, Bishopbriggs

a note about pocket canons

The Authorised King James Version of the Bible, translated between 1603–11, coincided with an extraordinary flowering of English literature. This version, more than any other, and possibly more than any other work in history, has had an influence in shaping the language we speak and write today.

Twenty-four of the eighty original books of the King James Bible are brought to you in this series. They encompass categories as diverse as history, philosophy, law, poetry and fiction. Each Pocket Canon also has its own introduction, specially commissioned from an impressive range of writers, to provide a personal interpretation of the text and explore its contemporary relevance.

introduction by joanna trollope

Author of eagerly awaited and bestselling novels often centred around the domestic nuances and dilemmas of life in contemporary England, Joanna Trollope is also the author of a number of histori-cal novels and of Britannica's Daughters, *a study of women in the British Empire. In 1988 she wrote her first contemporary novel,* The Choir, *and this was followed by* A Village Affair, A Pas-sionate Man, The Rector's Wife, The Men and the Girls, A Spanish Lover, The Best of Friends, Next of Kin *and most recently,* Other People's Children. *She lives in Gloucestershire.*

At first glance, it would seem natural, perhaps, to pair off the books of *Ruth* and *Esther* since they are the only two books in the Old Testament with women as their central characters, their heroines. At even a second glance, it might be tempting to see the two stories as applauding the courage and fortitude of women, a kind of remarkable early accolade to feminism. But a third glance reveals the reality. These two stories may *star* women, but only against the conventional biblical background of supreme male power; and if the women are celebrated, it is merely because of their ingenuity in exploiting that power. We are dealing it seems, with tradi-tional, accepted romantic heroines – except that we are not.

Love may come into both stories, lust even, but the loyalties the women in these stories show is most fiercely directed in the one case to another, older woman, and in the second case, to a race, to a people. If these women had merely been feisty examples of romantic femininity, they would not have taken such a hold as they have, on Jewish and Christian minds and hearts down the ages. It is their breadth and their differences that have given them their enduring power.

There are thirty-nine books in the King James Old Testament, from the first book of Moses, called *Genesis*, to *Malachi*. In most bibles, this works out at about a thousand pages. And for the first five hundred pages, we know roughly where we are; not just following the revelation of God's will and purpose for mankind, but also pursuing the extraordinary story of the rise and fall of the nation of Israel, from the call of Abraham to the point in the fourth century BC when the Jews eventually emerged as a distinct religious community settled in a tiny corner of the Persian Empire.

So far, so reasonably manageable. But after the book of *Nehemiah*, the pattern disappears. The continuity of the story fragments and diffuses into something different and less accessible – into the (very broadly speaking) literature of the Hebrew people, into their prophecies and poetry, their wisdom and stories. Instead of reading the books of the Old Testament in sequence, we can read them individually. They aren't exactly random but they aren't, because of their separate natures, in narrative or development of thought order, either.

Some books, like those of the prophets, illuminate the

history that has gone before as well as foretell the future. Some, like *Psalms*, from which hymns were used in Temple services, describe the nature and mood of Jewish worship after the exile of its people. And some – *Ruth* and *Esther* among them – are stories that, for various reasons, plainly became interwoven into Jewish life and faith, into its attitudes as well as its rituals.

Like all stories – at least stories that endure – the stories of *Ruth* and *Esther* are metaphors. At one level they are simple narratives – one romantic, one dramatic – but at another they are illustrations, or images, of human behaviour, human attitudes, human arbitrariness, human trial and error, human failing, human (with divine assistance) triumph. We may not be able to identify with the time and place, but in some way, however small, we can identify with some aspect of the human condition.

They are also in violent contrast to one another. *Ruth* is a story of simplicity and gentleness; *Esther* one of hatred and savagery. Both books were of course written pre-Christ, but only the book of *Ruth*, with its quiet virtues, its extolling of compassion and tolerance and honourable conduct, found favour with later Christian thinking. The name of God is invoked, called upon and blessed. *Esther*, on the other hand, never even mentions the name of God. Yet both have their place, and particular point, in this rich and amazing history of a remarkable people and their remarkable faith.

The book of *Ruth*, in the authorised version, now sits between *Judges* and the first book of *Samuel*. The Greek translators put it there because there is reference, in the first chapter, to the story having taken place 'in the days when the judges ruled'. It could have been written before the Exile (598 BC), it could have been written some time after, but its exact date is nothing like as important as the question raised by the mere fact of its inclusion in the first place. It's a charming story, certainly, with an equally charming, peaceful, pastoral setting, among the Bethlehem barley fields at harvest time (a welcome relief after all the blood and thunder of *Judges*). But it's also something more significant and more muscular because it suggests that not all Jews of the period believed in the remorselessly tough racial laws that followed their return from exile – the ban on mixed marriage, the segregation of their people from any other, the open hostility to foreigners.

Ruth, you see, is not a Jew. She is a Moabitess. She marries a Jew who has come to live in Moabite country and, after his death, makes her immortal speech to her Jewish mother-in-law, Naomi: 'Whither thou goest, I will go; and where thou lodgest, I will lodge; thy people shall be my people and thy God my God; where thou diest will I die and there I will be buried: The Lord do so to me and more also, if aught but death part thee and me'(1:16-17).

Naomi takes Ruth home to Bethlehem. To sustain them both, Naomi sends Ruth out to glean barley after the reapers – a privilege accorded to widows and the poor – in a kinsman's field. 'Whose', demands the immediately interested kinsman, 'damsel is this?' Soon, after some delicate moonlight manoeuvrings, she is his, Moabite or not. And soon again, she, as his wife, bears him a son. The son is named

Obed. Obed was the father of Jesse who in turn was the father of the great king, David. And the great King David – honoured almost as much as Moses – was the grandson, not just of Obed, but naturally of his wife too, who was a Gentile. It is as if the storyteller of *Ruth* is saying, gently but firmly, either that even the blood of the great king was diluted or – more likely – that God's chosen people must make room for others who truly wish to join them, such as Moabites and other Gentiles.

This tiny hint of racial intolerance is the only link between the tender book of *Ruth* and the fierce book of *Esther*; both the Jewish canon and the Christian church have expressed huge reluctance in accepting *Esther*, and Martin Luther bluntly wished it had never been written.

Their repugnance isn't hard to understand. It's a horrible story, a tale of hatred and massacre and revenge, and at the heart of it stands the beautiful Jewish consort of the Persian king, Xerxes I, remorselessly defending her people. In fact – again unlike Ruth – it hardly seems a suitable Biblical story at all.

It is, instead, like something from the *Tales of the Arabian Nights*. Xerxes, ruling a seething court in an opulent palace – the architecture and furnishings are described in lavish detail – is displeased at some minor (and understandable) disobedience on his wife's part. So he commands the land to be scoured for beautiful virgins and, of all of them, Esther, the foster-child and cousin of a Jew named Mordecai, finds supreme favour and becomes queen, without disclosing her religion. But the king's vizier, Haman, is deeply offended that

Mordecai 'bowed not, nor did him reverence', and orders him to be hanged, as a punishment, and also that all Jews around shall be slaughtered as a warning against further contemptuous behaviour.

Only the queen, revealing her race to the besotted king, saves the day. And that should be the happy ending. But it isn't. Haman is hanged on his own gallows and the Jews rise up and massacre everyone who had intended to massacre them. Then they have a party in celebration, two days of 'feasting and gladness'. And, down the ages, that party has continued in these 'days of Purim', a festival when the Jewish people celebrate relief from their enemies '… the month which was turned unto them from sorrow to joy, and from mourning into a good day … days of feasting and joy, and of sending portions one to another, and gifts to the poor'(9:22).

I have read both books over and over. I can see every reason – Jewish, Christian, humanitarian – for including the book of *Ruth*. But the book of *Esther* is another matter altogether. It incorporates everything that we all know fights strenuously against all the charities and harmonies we strive to achieve. But perhaps, on reflection, that is the point of it – it is a fascinating, glittering, gaudy, alarming reminder of how we can be, how we too often are. *Esther* is darkness in a beguiling mask of light.

the book of ruth

Now it came to pass in the days when the judges ruled, that there was a famine in the land. And a certain man of Beth-lehem-judah went to sojourn in the country of Moab, he, and his wife, and his two sons. ²And the name of the man was Elimelech, and the name of his wife Naomi, and the name of his two sons Mahlon and Chilion, Ephrathites of Beth-lehem-judah. And they came into the country of Moab, and continued there. ³And Elimelech Naomi's husband died; and she was left, and her two sons. ⁴And they took them wives of the women of Moab; the name of the one was Orpah, and the name of the other Ruth: and they dwelled there about ten years. ⁵And Mahlon and Chilion died also both of them; and the woman was left of her two sons and her husband.

⁶Then she arose with her daughters in law, that she might return from the country of Moab, for she had heard in the country of Moab how that the Lord had visited his people in giving them bread. ⁷Wherefore she went forth out of the place where she was, and her two daughters in law with her; and they went on the way to return unto the land of Judah. ⁸And Naomi said unto her two daughters in law, 'Go, return each to her mother's house: the Lord deal kindly with you, as ye have dealt with the dead, and with me. ⁹ The Lord

grant you that ye may find rest, each of you in the house of her husband.' Then she kissed them; and they lifted up their voice, and wept. ¹⁰And they said unto her, 'Surely we will return with thee unto thy people.' ¹¹And Naomi said, 'Turn again, my daughters: why will ye go with me? Are there yet any more sons in my womb, that they may be your husbands? ¹²Turn again, my daughters, go your way; for I am too old to have an husband. If I should say, I have hope, if I should have an husband also to night, and should also bear sons, ¹³ would ye tarry for them till they were grown? Would ye stay for them from having husbands? Nay, my daughters; for it grieveth me much for your sakes that the hand of the Lord is gone out against me.' ¹⁴And they lifted up their voice, and wept again: and Orpah kissed her mother in law; but Ruth clave unto her. ¹⁵And she said, 'Behold, thy sister in law is gone back unto her people, and unto her gods: return thou after thy sister in law.' ¹⁶And Ruth said, 'Intreat me not to leave thee, or to return from following after thee: for whither thou goest, I will go; and where thou lodgest, I will lodge: thy people shall be my people, and thy God my God: ¹⁷where thou diest, will I die, and there will I be buried: the Lord do so to me, and more also, if ought but death part thee and me.' ¹⁸ When she saw that she was stedfastly minded to go with her, then she left speaking unto her.

¹⁹ So they two went until they came to Beth-lehem. And it came to pass, when they were come to Beth-lehem, that all the city was moved about them, and they said, 'Is this Naomi?' ²⁰And she said unto them, 'Call me not Naomi, call me Mara:

for the Almighty hath dealt very bitterly with me. ²¹I went out full, and the Lord hath brought me home again empty: why then call ye me Naomi, seeing the Lord hath testified against me, and the Almighty hath afflicted me?' ²²So Naomi returned, and Ruth the Moabitess, her daughter in law, with her, which returned out of the country of Moab: and they came to Beth-lehem in the beginning of barley harvest.

2 And Naomi had a kinsman of her husband's, a mighty man of wealth, of the family of Elimelech; and his name was Boaz. ²And Ruth the Moabitess said unto Naomi, 'Let me now go to the field, and glean ears of corn after him in whose sight I shall find grace.' And she said unto her, 'Go, my daughter.' ³And she went, and came, and gleaned in the field after the reapers: and her hap was to light on a part of the field belonging unto Boaz, who was of the kindred of Elimelech.

⁴And, behold, Boaz came from Beth-lehem, and said unto the reapers, 'The Lord be with you.' And they answered him, 'The Lord bless thee.' ⁵Then said Boaz unto his servant that was set over the reapers, 'Whose damsel is this?' ⁶And the servant that was set over the reapers answered and said, 'It is the Moabitish damsel that came back with Naomi out of the country of Moab. ⁷And she said, 'I pray you, let me glean and gather after the reapers among the sheaves': so she came, and hath continued even from the morning until now, that she tarried a little in the house.' ⁸Then said Boaz unto Ruth, 'Hearest thou not, my daughter? Go not to glean in another field, neither go from hence, but abide here fast by my maidens. ⁹Let thine eyes be on the field that they do reap, and go thou after them: have I not charged the young men that they shall not touch thee? And when thou art athirst, go unto the vessels, and drink of that which the young men have drawn.' ¹⁰Then she fell on her face, and bowed herself to the ground, and said unto him, 'Why have I found grace in thine eyes, that thou shouldest take knowledge of me, seeing I am

tranger?' "And Boaz answered and said unto her, 'It hath ully been shewed me, all that thou hast done unto thy mother in law since the death of thine husband: and how hou hast left thy father and thy mother, and the land of thy ativity, and art come unto a people which thou knewest not eretofore.' ¹²The Lord recompense thy work, and a full eward be given thee of the Lord God of Israel, under whose vings thou art come to trust. ¹³Then she said, 'Let me find avour in thy sight, my lord; for that thou hast comforted ne, and for that thou hast spoken friendly unto thine hand-maid, though I be not like unto one of thine handmaidens.' And Boaz said unto her, 'At mealtime come thou hither, and at of the bread, and dip thy morsel in the vinegar.' And she at beside the reapers: and he reached her parched corn, and ne did eat, and was sufficed, and left. ¹⁵And when she was sen up to glean, Boaz commanded his young men, saying, et her glean even among the sheaves, and reproach her ot. ¹⁶And let fall also some of the handfuls of purpose for er, and leave them, that she may glean them, and rebuke er not.' ¹⁷So she gleaned in the field until even, and beat out at she had gleaned: and it was about an ephah of barley.

¹⁸And she took it up, and went into the city: and her mother in law saw what she had gleaned: and she brought orth, and gave to her that she had reserved after she was ufficed. ¹⁹And her mother in law said unto her, 'Where hast ou gleaned to day? And where wroughtest thou? Blessed e he that did take knowledge of thee.' And she shewed her mother in law with whom she had wrought, and said, 'The

man's name with whom I wrought to day is Boaz.' ²⁰And Naomi said unto her daughter in law, 'Blessed be he of the Lord, who hath not left off his kindness to the living and to the dead.' And Naomi said unto her, 'The man is near of kin unto us, one of our next kinsmen.' ²¹And Ruth the Moabites said, 'He said unto me also, "Thou shalt keep fast by my young men, until they have ended all my harvest."' ²²And Naomi said unto Ruth her daughter in law, 'It is good, my daughter, that thou go out with his maidens, that they meet thee not in any other field.' ²³So she kept fast by the maidens of Boaz to glean unto the end of barley harvest and of wheat harvest; and dwelt with her mother in law.

3 Then Naomi her mother in law said unto her, 'My daughter, shall I not seek rest for thee, that it may be well with thee? ²And now is not Boaz of our kindred, with whose maidens thou wast? Behold, he winnoweth barley to night in the threshingfloor. ³Wash thyself therefore, and anoint thee, and put thy raiment upon thee, and get thee down to the floor; but make not thyself known unto the man, until he shall have done eating and drinking. ⁴And it shall be, when he lieth down, that thou shalt mark the place where he shall lie, and thou shalt go in, and uncover his feet, and lay thee down; and he will tell thee what thou shalt do.' ⁵And she said unto her, 'All that thou sayest unto me I will do.'

⁶And she went down unto the floor, and did according to all that her mother in law bade her. ⁷And when Boaz had eaten and drunk, and his heart was merry, he went to lie down at the end of the heap of corn: and she came softly, and uncovered his feet, and laid her down.

⁸And it came to pass at midnight, that the man was afraid, and turned himself: and, behold, a woman lay at his feet. ⁹And he said, 'Who art thou?' And she answered, 'I am Ruth thine handmaid: spread therefore thy skirt over thine handmaid; for thou art a near kinsman.' ¹⁰And he said, 'Blessed be thou of the Lord, my daughter, for thou hast shewed more kindness in the latter end than at the beginning, inasmuch as thou followedst not young men, whether poor or rich. ¹¹And now, my daughter, fear not; I will do to thee all that thou requirest; for all the city of my people doth

know that thou art a virtuous woman. ¹²And now it is true that I am thy near kinsman: howbeit there is a kinsman nearer than I. ¹³Tarry this night, and it shall be in the morning, that if he will perform unto thee the part of a kinsman, well; let him do the kinsman's part; but if he will not do the part of a kinsman to thee, then will I do the part of a kinsman to thee, as the Lord liveth: lie down until the morning.'

¹⁴And she lay at his feet until the morning: and she rose up before one could know another. And he said, 'Let it not be known that a woman came into the floor.' ¹⁵Also he said, 'Bring the vail that thou hast upon thee, and hold it.' And when she held it, he measured six measures of barley, and laid it on her: and she went into the city. ¹⁶And when she came to her mother in law, she said, 'Who art thou, my daughter?' And she told her all that the man had done to her. ¹⁷And she said, 'These six measures of barley gave he me; for he said to me, "Go not empty unto thy mother in law."' ¹⁸Then said she, 'Sit still, my daughter, until thou know how the matter will fall, for the man will not be in rest, until he have finished the thing this day.'

4 Then went Boaz up to the gate, and sat him down there: and, behold, the kinsman of whom Boaz spake came by; unto whom he said, 'Ho, such a one! Turn aside, sit down here.' And he turned aside, and sat down. ²And he took ten men of the elders of the city, and said, 'Sit ye down here.' And they sat down. ³And he said unto the kinsman, 'Naomi, that is come again out of the country of Moab, selleth a parcel of land, which was our brother Elimelech's. ⁴And I thought to advertise thee, saying, "Buy it before the inhabitants, and before the elders of my people. If thou wilt redeem it, redeem it; but if thou wilt not redeem it, then tell me, that I may know; for there is none to redeem it beside thee; and I am after thee."' And he said, 'I will redeem it.' ⁵Then said Boaz, 'What day thou buyest the field of the hand of Naomi, thou must buy it also of Ruth the Moabitess, the wife of the dead, to raise up the name of the dead upon his inheritance.'

⁶And the kinsman said, 'I cannot redeem it for myself, lest I mar mine own inheritance: redeem thou my right to thyself; for I cannot redeem it.' ⁷Now this was the manner in former time in Israel concerning redeeming and concerning changing, for to confirm all things; a man plucked off his shoe, and gave it to his neighbour; and this was a testimony in Israel. ⁸Therefore the kinsman said unto Boaz, 'Buy it for thee.' So he drew off his shoe.

⁹And Boaz said unto the elders, and unto all the people, Ye are witnesses this day, that I have bought all that was Elimelech's, and all that was Chilion's and Mahlon's, of the hand of Naomi. ¹⁰Moreover Ruth the Moabitess, the wife of

Mahlon, have I purchased to be my wife, to raise up the name of the dead upon his inheritance, that the name of the dead be not cut off from among his brethren, and from the gate of his place: ye are witnesses this day.' ¹¹And all the people that were in the gate, and the elders, said, 'We are witnesses. The Lord make the woman that is come into thine house like Rachel and like Leah, which two did build the house of Israel; and do thou worthily in Ephratah, and be famous in Beth-lehem. ¹²And let thy house be like the house of Pharez, whom Tamar bare unto Judah, of the seed which the Lord shall give thee of this young woman.'

¹³So Boaz took Ruth, and she was his wife: and when he went in unto her, the Lord gave her conception, and she bare a son. ¹⁴And the women said unto Naomi, 'Blessed be the Lord, which hath not left thee this day without a kinsman, that his name may be famous in Israel. ¹⁵And he shall be unto thee a restorer of thy life, and a nourisher of thine old age, for thy daughter in law, which loveth thee, which is better to thee than seven sons, hath born him.' ¹⁶And Naomi took the child, and laid it in her bosom, and became nurse unto it. ¹⁷And the women her neighbours gave it a name, saying, 'There is a son born to Naomi'; and they called his name Obed: he is the father of Jesse, the father of David.

¹⁸Now these are the generations of Pharez: Pharez begat Hezron, ¹⁹and Hezron begat Ram, and Ram begat Amminadab, ²⁰and Amminadab begat Nahshon, and Nahshon begat Salmon, ²¹and Salmon begat Boaz, and Boaz begat Obed, ²²and Obed begat Jesse, and Jesse begat David.

the book of esther

Now it came to pass in the days of Ahasuerus (this is Ahasuerus which reigned, from India even unto Ethispia, over
an hundred and seven and twenty provinces) ² that in those
days, when the king Ahasuerus sat on the throne of his kingdom, which was in Shushan the palace, ³ in the third year of
his reign, he made a feast unto all his princes and his servants; the power of Persia and Media, the nobles and princes
of the provinces, being before him, ⁴ then he shewed the
riches of his glorious kingdom and the honour of his excel-
lent majesty many days, even an hundred and fourscore
days. ⁵ And when these days were expired, the king made a
feast unto all the people that were present in Shushan the
palace, both unto great and small, seven days, in the court of
the garden of the king's palace, ⁶ where were white, green,
and blue, hangings, fastened with cords of fine linen and
purple to silver rings and pillars of marble: the beds were of
gold and silver, upon a pavement of red, and blue, and
white, and black, marble. ⁷ And they gave them drink in vessels of gold (the vessels being diverse one from another), and
royal wine in abundance, according to the state of the king.
⁸ And the drinking was according to the law; none did com-
pel: for so the king had appointed to all the officers of his

house, that they should do according to every man's pleasure. ⁹Also Vashti the queen made a feast for the women in the royal house which belonged to king Ahasuerus.

¹⁰On the seventh day, when the heart of the king was merry with wine, he commanded Mehuman, Biztha, Harbona, Bigtha, and Abagtha, Zethar, and Carcas, the seven chamberlains that served in the presence of Ahasuerus the king, ¹¹to bring Vashti the queen before the king with the crown royal, to shew the people and the princes her beauty, for she was fair to look on. ¹²But the queen Vashti refused to come at the king's commandment by his chamberlains: therefore was the king very wroth, and his anger burned in him.

¹³Then the king said to the wise men, which knew the times (for so was the king's manner toward all that knew law and judgment; ¹⁴and the next unto him was Carshena, Shethar, Admatha, Tarshish, Meres, Marsena, and Memucan, the seven princes of Persia and Media, which saw the king's face, and which sat the first in the kingdom), ¹⁵'What shall we do unto the queen Vashti according to law, because she hath not performed the commandment of the king Ahasuerus by the chamberlains?' ¹⁶And Memucan answered before the king and the princes, 'Vashti the queen hath not done wrong to the king only, but also to all the princes, and to all the people that are in all the provinces of the king Ahasuerus. ¹⁷For this deed of the queen shall come abroad unto all women, so that they shall despise their husbands in their eyes, when it shall be reported, "The king Ahasuerus commanded Vashti the queen to be brought in before him, but

she came not." ¹⁸ Likewise shall the ladies of Persia and Media say this day unto all the king's princes, which have heard of the deed of the queen. Thus shall there arise too much contempt and wrath. ¹⁹ If it please the king, let there go a royal commandment from him, and let it be written among the laws of the Persians and the Medes, that it be not altered, that Vashti come no more before king Ahasuerus; and let the king give her royal estate unto another that is better than she. ²⁰ And when the king's decree which he shall make shall be published throughout all his empire (for it is great), all the wives shall give to their husbands honour, both to great and small.' ²¹ And the saying pleased the king and the princes; and the king did according to the word of Memucan, ²² for he sent letters into all the king's provinces, into every province according to the writing thereof, and to every people after their language, that every man should bear rule in his own house, and that it should be published according to the language of every people.

2 After these things, when the wrath of king Ahasuerus was appeased, he remembered Vashti, and what she had done, and what was decreed against her. ²Then said the king's servants that ministered unto him, 'Let there be fair young virgins sought for the king: ³and let the king appoint officers in all the provinces of his kingdom, that they may gather together all the fair young virgins unto Shushan the palace, to the house of the women, unto the custody of Hege the king's chamberlain, keeper of the women; and let their things for purification be given them. ⁴And let the maiden which pleaseth the king be queen instead of Vashti.' And the thing pleased the king; and he did so.

⁵Now in Shushan the palace there was a certain Jew, whose name was Mordecai, the son of Jair, the son of Shimei, the son of Kish, a Benjamite, ⁶who had been carried away from Jerusalem with the captivity which had been carried away with Jeconiah king of Judah, whom Nebuchadnezzar the king of Babylon had carried away. ⁷And he brought up Hadassah, that is, Esther, his uncle's daughter, for she had neither father nor mother, and the maid was fair and beautiful, whom Mordecai, when her father and mother were dead, took for his own daughter.

⁸So it came to pass, when the king's commandment and his decree was heard, and when many maidens were gathered together unto Shushan the palace, to the custody of Hegai, that Esther was brought also unto the king's house, to the custody of Hegai, keeper of the women. ⁹And the maiden pleased him, and she obtained kindness of him; and he

speedily gave her her things for purification, with such things as belonged to her, and seven maidens, which were meet to be given her, out of the king's house: and he preferred her and her maids unto the best place of the house of the women. ¹⁰ Esther had not shewed her people nor her kindred, for Mordecai had charged her that she should not shew it. ¹¹And Mordecai walked every day before the court of the women's house, to know how Esther did, and what should become of her.

¹² Now when every maid's turn was come to go in to king Ahasuerus, after that she had been twelve months, according to the manner of the women (for so were the days of their purifications accomplished, to wit, six months with oil of myrrh, and six months with sweet odours, and with other things for the purifying of the women); ¹³ then thus came every maiden unto the king; whatsoever she desired was given her to go with her out of the house of the women unto the king's house. ¹⁴ In the evening she went, and on the morrow she returned into the second house of the women, to the custody of Shaashgaz, the king's chamberlain, which kept the concubines: she came in unto the king no more, except the king delighted in her, and that she were called by name.

¹⁵ Now when the turn of Esther, the daughter of Abihail the uncle of Mordecai, who had taken her for his daughter, was come to go in unto the king, she required nothing but what Hegai the king's chamberlain, the keeper of the women, appointed. And Esther obtained favour in the sight of all them that looked upon her. ¹⁶ So Esther was taken unto

king Ahasuerus into his house royal in the tenth month, which is the month Tebeth, in the seventh year of his reign. ¹⁷And the king loved Esther above all the women, and she obtained grace and favour in his sight more than all the virgins; so that he set the royal crown upon her head, and made her queen instead of Vashti. ¹⁸Then the king made a great feast unto all his princes and his servants, even Esther's feast; and he made a release to the provinces, and gave gifts, according to the state of the king. ¹⁹And when the virgins were gathered together the second time, then Mordecai sat in the king's gate. ²⁰Esther had not yet shewed her kindred nor her people, as Mordecai had charged her; for Esther did the commandment of Mordecai, like as when she was brought up with him.

²¹In those days, while Mordecai sat in the king's gate, two of the king's chamberlains, Bigthan and Teresh, of those which kept the door, were wroth, and sought to lay hand on the king Ahasuerus. ²²And the thing was known to Mordecai, who told it unto Esther the queen; and Esther certified the king thereof in Mordecai's name. ²³And when inquisition was made of the matter, it was found out; therefore they were both hanged on a tree; and it was written in the book of the chronicles before the king.

3 After these things did king Ahasuerus promote Haman the son of Hammedatha the Agagite, and advanced him, and set his seat above all the princes that were with him. ²And all the king's servants, that were in the king's gate, bowed, and reverenced Haman, for the king had so commanded concerning him. But Mordecai bowed not, nor did him reverence. ³Then the king's servants, which were in the king's gate, said unto Mordecai, 'Why transgressest thou the king's commandment?' ⁴Now it came to pass, when they spake daily unto him, and he hearkened not unto them, that they told Haman, to see whether Mordecai's matters would stand, for he had told them that he was a Jew.' ⁵And when Haman saw that Mordecai bowed not, nor did him reverence, then was Haman full of wrath. ⁶And he thought scorn to lay hands on Mordecai alone; for they had shewed him the people of Mordecai: wherefore Haman sought to destroy all the Jews that were throughout the whole kingdom of Ahasuerus, even the people of Mordecai.

⁷In the first month, that is, the month Nisan, in the twelfth year of king Ahasuerus, they cast Pur, that is, the lot, before Haman from day to day, and from month to month, to the twelfth month, that is, the month Adar.

⁸And Haman said unto king Ahasuerus, 'There is a certain people scattered abroad and dispersed among the people in all the provinces of thy kingdom; and their laws are diverse from all people; neither keep they the king's laws: therefore it is not for the king's profit to suffer them. ⁹If it please the king, let it be written that they may be destroyed: and I will

pay ten thousand talents of silver to the hands of those that have the charge of the business, to bring it into the king's treasuries.' ¹⁰And the king took his ring from his hand, and gave it unto Haman the son of Hammedatha the Agagite, the Jews' enemy. ¹¹And the king said unto Haman, 'The silver is given to thee, the people also, to do with them as it seemeth good to thee.' ¹²Then were the king's scribes called on the thirteenth day of the first month, and there was written according to all that Haman had commanded unto the king's lieutenants, and to the governors that were over every province, and to the rulers of every people of every province according to the writing thereof, and to every people after their language; in the name of king Ahasuerus was it written, and sealed with the king's ring. ¹³And the letters were sent by posts into all the king's provinces, to destroy, to kill, and to cause to perish, all Jews, both young and old, little children and women, in one day, even upon the thirteenth day of the twelfth month, which is the month Adar, and to take the spoil of them for a prey. ¹⁴The copy of the writing for a commandment to be given in every province was published unto all people, that they should be ready against that day. ¹⁵The posts went out, being hastened by the king's commandment, and the decree was given in Shushan the palace. And the king and Haman sat down to drink; but the city Shushan was perplexed.

4 When Mordecai perceived all that was done, Mordecai rent his clothes, and put on sackcloth with ashes, and went out into the midst of the city, and cried with a loud and a bitter cry; ²and came even before the king's gate, for none might enter into the king's gate clothed with sackcloth. ³And in every province, whithersoever the king's commandment and his decree came, there was great mourning among the Jews, and fasting, and weeping, and wailing; and many lay in sackcloth and ashes.

⁴So Esther's maids and her chamberlains came and told it her. Then was the queen exceedingly grieved; and she sent raiment to clothe Mordecai, and to take away his sackcloth from him: but he received it not. ⁵Then called Esther for Hatach, one of the king's chamberlains, whom he had appointed to attend upon her, and gave him a commandment to Mordecai, to know what it was, and why it was. ⁶So Hatach went forth to Mordecai unto the street of the city, which was before the king's gate. ⁷And Mordecai told him of all that had happened unto him, and of the sum of the money that Haman had promised to pay to the king's treasuries for the Jews, to destroy them. ⁸Also he gave him the copy of the writing of the decree that was given at Shushan to destroy them, to shew it unto Esther, and to declare it unto her, and to charge her that she should go in unto the king, to make supplication unto him, and to make request before him for her people. ⁹And Hatach came and told Esther the words of Mordecai.

¹⁰Again Esther spake unto Hatach, and gave him commandment unto Mordecai; ¹¹all the king's servants, and the

people of the king's provinces, do know, that whosoever, whether man or woman, shall come unto the king into the inner court, who is not called, there is one law of his to put him to death, except such to whom the king shall hold out the golden sceptre, that he may live; but I have not been called to come in unto the king these thirty days. ¹²And they told to Mordecai Esther's words. ¹³Then Mordecai commanded to answer Esther, 'Think not with thyself that thou shalt escape in the king's house, more than all the Jews. ¹⁴For if thou altogether holdest thy peace at this time, then shall there enlargement and deliverance arise to the Jews from another place; but thou and thy father's house shall be destroyed; and who knoweth whether thou art come to the kingdom for such a time as this?'

¹⁵Then Esther bade them return Mordecai this answer, ¹⁶'Go, gather together all the Jews that are present in Shushan, and fast ye for me, and neither eat nor drink three days, night or day: I also and my maidens will fast likewise; and so will I go in unto the king, which is not according to the law; and if I perish, I perish.' ¹⁷So Mordecai went his way, and did according to all that Esther had commanded him.

5 Now it came to pass on the third day, that Esther put on her royal apparel, and stood in the inner court of the king's house, over against the king's house; and the king sat upon his royal throne in the royal house, over against the gate of the house. ²And it was so, when the king saw Esther the queen standing in the court, that she obtained favour in his sight: and the king held out to Esther the golden sceptre that was in his hand. So Esther drew near, and touched the top of the sceptre. ³Then said the king unto her, 'What wilt thou, queen Esther? And what is thy request? It shall be even given thee to the half of the kingdom.' ⁴And Esther answered, 'If it seem good unto the king, let the king and Haman come this day unto the banquet that I have prepared for him.' ⁵Then the king said, 'Cause Haman to make haste, that he may do as Esther hath said.' So the king and Haman came to the banquet that Esther had prepared.

⁶And the king said unto Esther at the banquet of wine, 'What is thy petition? And it shall be granted thee: and what is thy request? Even to the half of the kingdom it shall be performed.' ⁷Then answered Esther, and said, 'My petition and my request is: ⁸ if I have found favour in the sight of the king, and if it please the king to grant my petition, and to perform my request, let the king and Haman come to the banquet that I shall prepare for them, and I will do to morrow as the king hath said.'

⁹Then went Haman forth that day joyful and with a glad heart; but when Haman saw Mordecai in the king's gate, that he stood not up, nor moved for him, he was full

of indignation against Mordecai. ¹⁰ Nevertheless Haman refrained himself: and when he came home, he sent and called for his friends, and Zeresh his wife. ¹¹And Haman told them of the glory of his riches, and the multitude of his children, and all the things wherein the king had promoted him, and how he had advanced him above the princes and servants of the king. ¹²Haman said moreover, 'Yea, Esther the queen did let no man come in with the king unto the banquet that she had prepared but myself; and to morrow am I invited unto her also with the king. ¹³Yet all this availeth me nothing, so long as I see Mordecai the Jew sitting at the king's gate.'

¹⁴Then said Zeresh his wife and all his friends unto him, 'Let a gallows be made of fifty cubits high, and to morrow speak thou unto the king that Mordecai may be hanged thereon: then go thou in merrily with the king unto the banquet.' And the thing pleased Haman; and he caused the gallows to be made.

6 On that night could not the king sleep, and he commanded to bring the book of records of the chronicles; and they were read before the king. ²And it was found written, that Mordecai had told of Bigthana and Teresh, two of the king's chamberlains, the keepers of the door, who sought to lay hand on the king Ahasuerus. ³And the king said, 'What honour and dignity hath been done to Mordecai for this?' Then said the king's servants that ministered unto him, 'There is nothing done for him.'

⁴And the king said, 'Who is in the court?' Now Haman was come into the outward court of the king's house, to speak unto the king to hang Mordecai on the gallows that he had prepared for him. ⁵And the king's servants said unto him, 'Behold, Haman standeth in the court.' And the king said, 'Let him come in.' ⁶So Haman came in. And the king said unto him, 'What shall be done unto the man whom the king delighteth to honour?' Now Haman thought in his heart, 'To whom would the king delight to do honour more than to myself?' ⁷And Haman answered the king, 'For the man whom the king delighteth to honour, ⁸let the royal apparel be brought which the king useth to wear, and the horse that the king rideth upon, and the crown royal which is set upon his head. ⁹And let this apparel and horse be delivered to the hand of one of the king's most noble princes, that they may array the man withal whom the king delighteth to honour, and bring him on horseback through the street of the city, and proclaim before him, "Thus shall it be done to the man whom the king delighteth to honour."'

[10] Then the king said to Haman, 'Make haste, and take the apparel and the horse, as thou hast said, and do even so to Mordecai the Jew, that sitteth at the king's gate: let nothing fail of all that thou hast spoken.' [11] Then took Haman the apparel and the horse, and arrayed Mordecai, and brought him on horseback through the street of the city, and proclaimed before him, 'Thus shall it be done unto the man whom the king delighteth to honour.'

[12] And Mordecai came again to the king's gate. But Haman hasted to his house mourning, and having his head covered. [13] And Haman told Zeresh his wife and all his friends every thing that had befallen him. Then said his wise men and Zeresh his wife unto him, 'If Mordecai be of the seed of the Jews, before whom thou hast begun to fall, thou shalt not prevail against him, but shalt surely fall before him.' [14] And while they were yet talking with him, came the king's chamberlains, and hasted to bring Haman unto the banquet that Esther had prepared.

7 So the king and Haman came to banquet with Esther the queen. ²And the king said again unto Esther on the second day at the banquet of wine, 'What is thy petition, queen Esther? And it shall be granted thee: and what is thy request? And it shall be performed, even to the half of the kingdom.' ³Then Esther the queen answered and said, 'If I have found favour in thy sight, O king, and if it please the king, let my life be given me at my petition, and my people at my request, ⁴for we are sold, I and my people, to be destroyed, to be slain, and to perish. But if we had been sold for bondmen and bondwomen, I had held my tongue, although the enemy could not countervail the king's damage.'

⁵Then the king Ahasuerus answered and said unto Esther the queen, 'Who is he, and where is he, that durst presume in his heart to do so?' ⁶And Esther said, 'The adversary and enemy is this wicked Haman.' Then Haman was afraid before the king and the queen.

⁷And the king arising from the banquet of wine in his wrath went into the palace garden: and Haman stood up to make request for his life to Esther the queen; for he saw that there was evil determined against him by the king. ⁸Then the king returned out of the palace garden into the place of the banquet of wine; and Haman was fallen upon the bed whereon Esther was. Then said the king, 'Will he force the queen also before me in the house?' As the word went out of the king's mouth, they covered Haman's face. ⁹And Harbonah, one of the chamberlains, said before the king, 'Behold also, the gallows fifty cubits high, which

Haman had made for Mordecai, who had spoken good for the king, standeth in the house of Haman.' Then the king said, 'Hang him thereon.' ¹⁰ So they hanged Haman on the gallows that he had prepared for Mordecai. Then was the king's wrath pacified.

8 On that day did the king Ahasuerus give the house of Haman the Jews' enemy unto Esther the queen. And Mordecai came before the king; for Esther had told what he was unto her. ²And the king took off his ring, which he had taken from Haman, and gave it unto Mordecai. And Esther set Mordecai over the house of Haman.

³And Esther spake yet again before the king, and fell down at his feet, and besought him with tears to put away the mischief of Haman the Agagite, and his device that he had devised against the Jews. ⁴Then the king held out the golden sceptre toward Esther. So Esther arose, and stood before the king. ⁵And said, 'If it please the king, and if I have found favour in his sight, and the thing seem right before the king, and I be pleasing in his eyes, let it be written to reverse the letters devised by Haman the son of Hammedatha the Agagite, which he wrote to destroy the Jews which are in all the king's provinces. ⁶For how can I endure to see the evil that shall come unto my people? or how can I endure to see the destruction of my kindred?'

⁷Then the king Ahasuerus said unto Esther the queen and to Mordecai the Jew, 'Behold, I have given Esther the house of Haman, and him they have hanged upon the gallows, because he laid his hand upon the Jews. ⁸Write ye also for the Jews, as it liketh you, in the king's name, and seal it with the king's ring, for the writing which is written in the king's name, and sealed with the king's ring, may no man reverse.' ⁹Then were the king's scribes called at that time in the third month, that is, the month Sivan, on the three and

twentieth day thereof; and it was written according to all that Mordecai commanded unto the Jews, and to the lieutenants, and the deputies and rulers of the provinces which are from India unto Ethiopia, an hundred twenty and seven provinces, unto every province according to the writing thereof, and unto every people after their language, and to the Jews according to their writing, and according to their language. ¹⁰And he wrote in the king Ahasuerus' name, and sealed it with the king's ring, and sent letters by posts on horseback, and riders on mules, camels, and young dromedaries: ¹¹wherein the king granted the Jews which were in every city to gather themselves together, and to stand for their life, to destroy, to slay, and to cause to perish, all the power of the people and province that would assault them, both little ones and women, and to take the spoil of them for a prey, ¹²upon one day in all the provinces of king Ahasuerus, namely, upon the thirteenth day of the twelfth month, which is the month Adar. ¹³The copy of the writing for a commandment to be given in every province was published unto all people, and that the Jews should be ready against that day to avenge themselves on their enemies. ¹⁴So the posts that rode upon mules and camels went out, being hastened and pressed on by the king's commandment. And the decree was given at Shushan the palace.

¹⁵And Mordecai went out from the presence of the king in royal apparel of blue and white, and with a great crown of gold, and with a garment of fine linen and purple: and the city of Shushan rejoiced and was glad. ¹⁶The Jews had light,

and gladness, and joy, and honour. [17]And in every province, and in every city, whithersoever the king's commandment and his decree came, the Jews had joy and gladness, a feast and a good day. And many of the people of the land became Jews; for the fear of the Jews fell upon them.

9 Now in the twelfth month, that is, the month Adar, on the thirteenth day of the same, when the king's commandment and his decree drew near to be put in execution, in the day that the enemies of the Jews hoped to have power over them (though it was turned to the contrary, that the Jews had rule over them that hated them), ²the Jews gathered themselves together in their cities throughout all the provinces of the king Ahasuerus, to lay hand on such as sought their hurt; and no man could withstand them, for the fear of them fell upon all people. ³And all the rulers of the provinces, and the lieutenants, and the deputies, and officers of the king, helped the Jews; because the fear of Mordecai fell upon them. ⁴For Mordecai was great in the king's house, and his fame went out throughout all the provinces; for this man Mordecai waxed greater and greater. ⁵Thus the Jews smote all their enemies with the stroke of the sword, and slaughter, and destruction, and did what they would unto those that hated them. ⁶And in Shushan the palace the Jews slew and destroyed five hundred men. ⁷And Parshandatha, and Dalphon, and Aspatha, ⁸and Poratha, and Adalia, and Aridatha, ⁹and Parmashta, and Arisai, and Aridai, and Vajezatha, ¹⁰the ten sons of Haman the son of Hammedatha, the enemy of the Jews, slew they; but on the spoil laid they not their hand. ¹¹On that day the number of those that were slain in Shushan the palace was brought before the king.

¹²And the king said unto Esther the queen, 'The Jews have slain and destroyed five hundred men in Shushan the

palace, and the ten sons of Haman; what have they done in the rest of the king's provinces? Now what is thy petition? And it shall be granted thee: or what is thy request further? And it shall be done. ¹³ Then said Esther, 'If it please the king, let it be granted to the Jews which are in Shushan to do to morrow also according unto this day's decree, and let Haman's ten sons be hanged upon the gallows.' ¹⁴And the king commanded it so to be done; and the decree was given at Shushan; and they hanged Haman's ten sons. ¹⁵ For the Jews that were in Shushan gathered themselves together on the fourteenth day also of the month Adar, and slew three hundred men at Shushan; but on the prey they laid not their hand. ¹⁶ But the other Jews that were in the king's provinces gathered themselves together, and stood for their lives, and had rest from their enemies, and slew of their foes seventy and five thousand, but they laid not their hands on the prey, ¹⁷on the thirteenth day of the month Adar; and on the fourteenth day of the same rested they, and made it a day of feasting and gladness. ¹⁸ But the Jews that were at Shushan assembled together on the thirteenth day thereof, and on the fourteenth thereof; and on the fifteenth day of the same they rested, and made it a day of feasting and gladness. ¹⁹ Therefore the Jews of the villages, that dwelt in the unwalled towns, made the fourteenth day of the month Adar a day of gladness and feasting, and a good day, and of sending portions one to another.

²⁰And Mordecai wrote these things, and sent letters unto all the Jews that were in all the provinces of the king

Ahasuerus, both nigh and far, ²¹ to stablish this among them, that they should keep the fourteenth day of the month Adar, and the fifteenth day of the same, yearly, ²² as the days wherein the Jews rested from their enemies, and the month which was turned unto them from sorrow to joy, and from mourning into a good day, that they should make them days of feasting and joy, and of sending portions one to another, and gifts to the poor. ²³ And the Jews undertook to do as they had begun, and as Mordecai had written unto them, ²⁴ because Haman the son of Hammedatha, the Agagite, the enemy of all the Jews, had devised against the Jews to destroy them, and had cast Pur, that is, the lot, to consume them, and to destroy them; ²⁵ but when Esther came before the king, he commanded by letters that his wicked device, which he devised against the Jews, should return upon his own head, and that he and his sons should be hanged on the gallows. ²⁶ Wherefore they called these days Purim after the name of Pur. Therefore for all the words of this letter, and of that which they had seen concerning this matter, and which had come unto them, ²⁷ the Jews ordained, and took upon them, and upon their seed, and upon all such as joined themselves unto them, so as it should not fail, that they would keep these two days according to their writing, and according to their appointed time every year; ²⁸ and that these days should be remembered and kept throughout every generation, every family, every province, and every city; and that these days of Purim should not fail from among the Jews, nor the memorial of them perish from their seed. ²⁹ Then Esther the queen, the daughter of Abihail, and Mordecai the Jew, wrote with all authority, to confirm this second letter of Purim. ³⁰ And he sent the letters unto all the Jews, to the hundred twenty and seven provinces of the kingdom of Ahasuerus, with words of peace and truth, ³¹ to confirm these days of Purim in their times appointed, according as Mordecai the Jew and Esther the queen had enjoined them, and as they had decreed for themselves and for their seed, the matters of the fastings and their cry. ³² And the decree of Esther confirmed these matters of Purim; and it was written in the book.

10 And the king Ahasuerus laid a tribute upon the land, and upon the isles of the sea. ²And all the acts of his power and of his might, and the declaration of the greatness of Mordecai, whereunto the king advanced him, are they not written in the book of the chronicles of the kings of Media and Persia? ³For Mordecai the Jew was next unto king Ahasuerus, and great among the Jews, and accepted of the multitude of his brethren, seeking the wealth of his people, and speaking peace to all his seed.

the pocket canons

All of the above titles can be ordered directly from:
Canongate Books, 14 High Street, Edinburgh EH1 1TE
Tel 0131 557 5111   Fax 0131 557 5211